LUNCHBOX

CONTENTS

LUNCHTIME

It is important to have a meal in the middle of the day. Lunch gives the body everything it needs to keep it working properly through the afternoon.

Many people take a sandwich lunch with them to school or work.

The best way to carry sandwiches is in a lunchbox. A lunchbox stops any food inside being squashed. It also keeps sandwiches fresh and dry.

Everything we use and eat is changed in some way before it gets to us. Bread, butter, cheese, apples and even plastic lunchboxes go through different processes. This book will tell you about these **processes**.

BREAD

FROM WHEAT TO FLOUR

Bread is the main part of a sandwich. It is made from flour. The flour comes from wheat.

At harvest time the wheat grain is collected and stored in a barn. The wheat is then dried to stop it going mouldy. Hot air is blown through the grain. The dry grain is stored in large grain bins. Some of the grain will be kept for sowing next year. Most of it is taken to a mill to be ground up into flour.

At the mill the grain is cleaned. Then it is crushed between rollers. The crushed grain is sieved, to separate the different parts of the wheat grains.

- White flour is made from just **endosperm**.

- Brown flour is made from endosperm, **wheat germ** and a little **bran**.

- Wholemeal flour has all three parts of the grain in it.

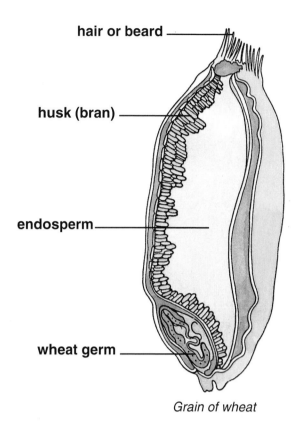

Grain of wheat

(**2**) *Then it is crushed between rollers.*

(**3**) *The crushed grain is sieved to separate the different parts of the wheat grain.*

FROM WHEAT TO FLOUR

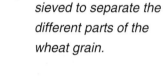

(**1**) *At the mill the grain is cleaned.*

(**4**) *The finished white flour.*

Dirt removed from wheat.

MAKING BREAD

At the bakery the flour is put into a large bowl with water, salt and **yeast**. The mixture is stirred by a machine. It turns into a pale grey lump called **dough**

water

flour

salt

yeast

Then the dough is left to stand for about an hour. The yeast inside the dough grows and makes bubbles. The bubbles make the dough double in size.

The dough is then cut up and put into tins.

The tins are stored in warm cupboards for about half an hour. The heat in the cupboards makes the yeast grow even more, so the dough rises even higher.

The risen dough is put in a hot oven for about 20 minutes. The heat does three things. It kills the yeast. It swells the bubbles to make the dough rise even more, and it bakes the dough to make bread.

When the bread comes out of the oven it is cooled before it is ready for sale. In large bakeries the bread is sliced and packed in plastic bags to keep it fresh on its way to the supermarket. In smaller bakeries it is put on to the shop shelves and sold in paper bags.

DIFFERENT KINDS OF BREAD

There are many different kinds of bread. Different processes are used to make them. They are made from different kinds of flour. Some kinds of bread have extra ingredients.

French bread is made from a special type of white flour which can be bought in France.

Naan bread is made from white flour, eggs and yoghurt. It is flat like pitta bread.

Pitta bread is made from brown or white flour and is flatter than most bread.

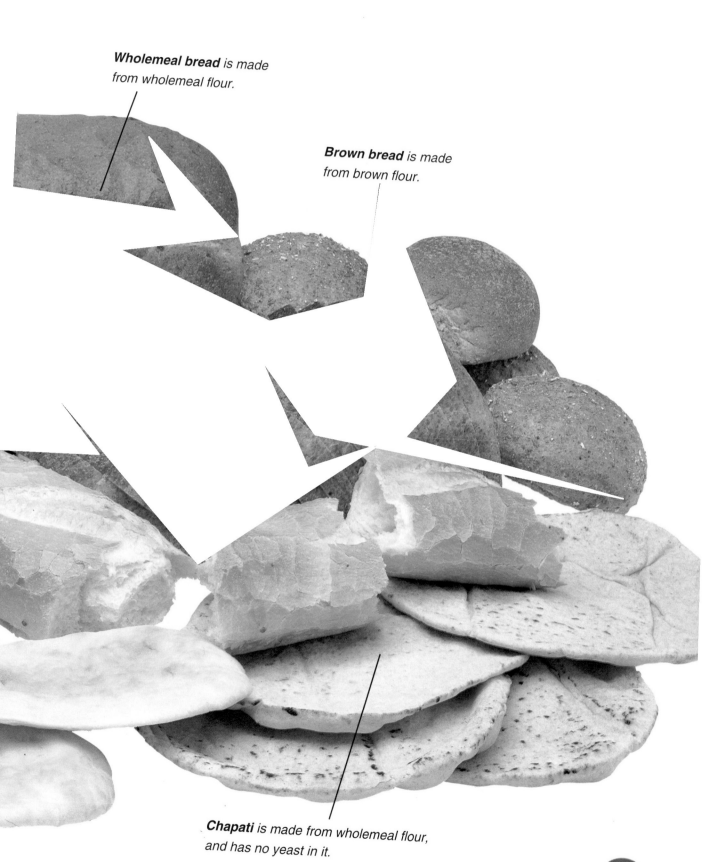

Wholemeal bread is made from wholemeal flour.

Brown bread is made from brown flour.

Chapati is made from wholemeal flour, and has no yeast in it.

BUTTER

SEPARATING THE MILK AND CREAM

Butter is made from cream. Cream comes from milk. At the dairy, full-cream milk from the farm is put into a cream separator. The milk spins round inside this machine. There are holes in the machine. The milk splashes through the holes but the cream stays inside. The cream can then be made into butter. The left over milk is called **skimmed milk**.

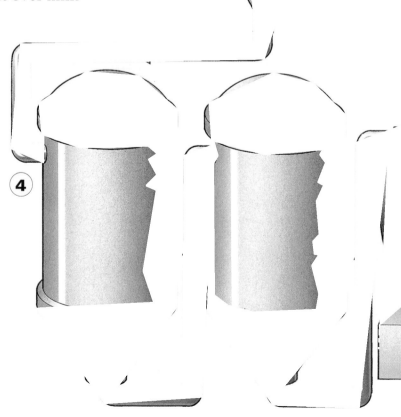

1 full-cream milk in

2 skimmed milk out

3 cream in

4

cream treatment unit

MAKING BUTTER

The butter is made by a butter-making machine. Cream is pumped into one end of it. First the cream is heated and then cooled. The cool cream is left for about twelve hours. Then it is shaken. Shaken cream changes into lumps of butter and watery milk called buttermilk.

The buttermilk flows away from the lumps of butter. The lumps of butter are washed with water. They are squashed together with salt to make a slab of butter. The salt makes the butter stay fresh longer. Long strips of butter are pushed out at the other end. The butter is cut up into blocks and wrapped in paper or foil.

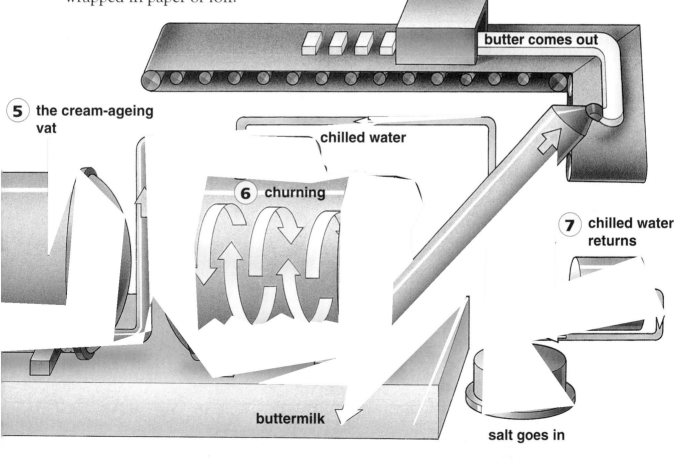

butter comes out

5 the cream-ageing vat

chilled water

6 churning

7 chilled water returns

buttermilk

salt goes in

CHEESE

SEPARATING THE CURDS AND WHEY

Cheese is made from full-cream milk. At the factory this milk is mixed with skimmed milk which contains bacteria that make acid. The mixture is kept warm. Soon the milk thickens up and turns sour.

A **chemical** called **rennilase** is added. The sour milk is kept warm and the rennilase changes it into big lumps called curds.

Some of the milk inside the curds turns watery. This watery milk is called whey. The curds are cut up to let the whey flow out.

MAKING CHEESE

Salt is added to the curds, then they are squeezed in a cheese press.

The curds are put into **moulds** and left in a cool place for a few months. They turn into cheese. The cheese is cut up into blocks.

Sometimes it is packed in tight-fitting clear plastic to be sold in supermarkets. Sometimes it is packaged in different ways.

DIFFERENT KINDS OF CHEESE

There are many different kinds of cheese, from all over the world.

Edam is a popular Dutch cheese with a red rind.

Cheddar is the most popular English cheese. It has a nutty flavour.

Brie is a creamy French cheese.

Parmesan is an Italian cheese which is put on spaghetti and other dishes.

Stilton is an English cheese with patches of blue mould in it for extra flavour.

Mozarella is an Italian cheese that is used in pizza toppings.

Some English cheeses are named after the place where they were first made.

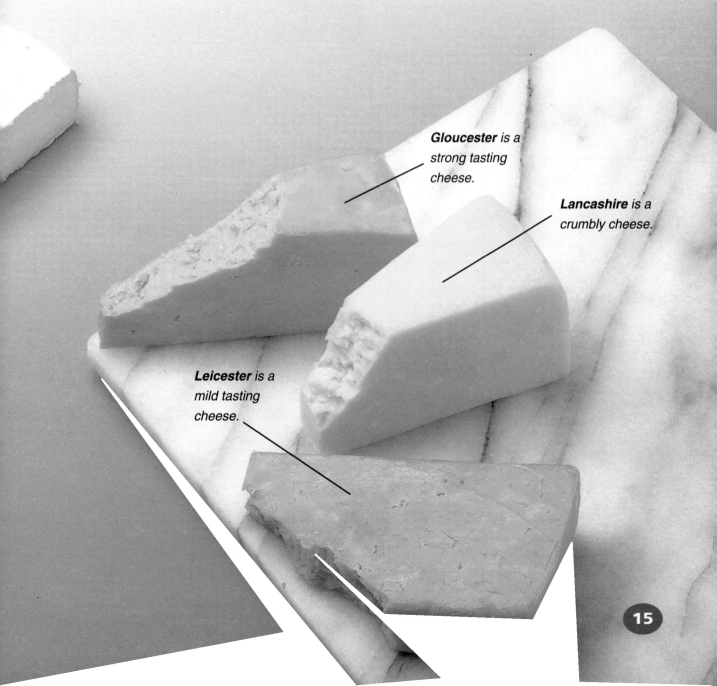

Gloucester *is a strong tasting cheese.*

Lancashire *is a crumbly cheese.*

Leicester *is a mild tasting cheese.*

APPLES

THE ORCHARD

The place where apple trees are grown is called an orchard.

The flowers of an apple tree are called blossom. The apples grow from them.

The middle of the apple flower swells up to make the apple.

The other parts of the flower fall away leaving the apple on the twig.

As the apples grow, farmers spray them with **pesticide**.
The pesticide kills black scab and codling moths.

Black scab is a **fungus** that grows on apple skin.

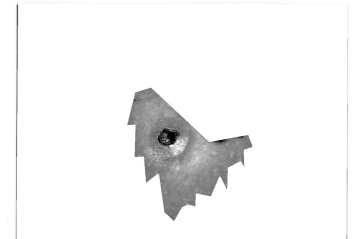

The larva of the codling moth is a 'maggot' that burrows its way inside the apple.

HARVEST TIME

By the end of the summer the apples
are ripe. This means the apples have
swollen up to their full size and may
have changed colour. When the stalks
of the ripe apples become weak they
are ready for picking. Apples are picked
by hand because they bruise easily.

The apples are collected into bins and stored until they are
sold. So many apples are produced in the autumn that it may
be months before they are sold. The apples are stored in a
cool place and sprayed with more pesticide to stop them
going rotten.

*Cox's Oran
Pippin*

READY FOR MARKET

The apples are washed and sorted.

Then they are checked and wrapped. The wrapping stops the apples being bruised as they are taken from the orchards to the shops.

Some shops sell the apples in plastic bags.

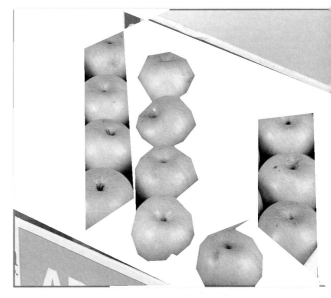

DIFFERENT KINDS OF APPLE

Golden Delicious

Red Delicious

Granny Smith

THE LUNCHBOX

The plastic lunchbox is made from **polythene**.

(1) The white chips of polythene are poured into a moulding machine. They are pushed through the machine by a metal rod called a ram.

(2) As they go through the machine the chips are heated. They melt together and turn into a liquid.

(3) The liquid is squeezed through a pipe into a mould. The mould is in the shape of the lunchbox.

(4) The mould is cooled by water and the liquid plastic turns into a solid again. It sets in the shape of the lunchbox.

(5) The plastic lunchbox is taken out of the mould. The stump where the plastic in the pipe joined the mould is cut off.

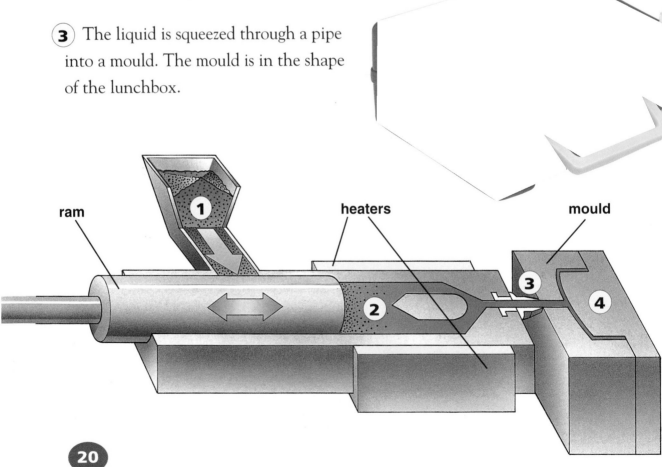

ram   heaters   mould

A HEALTHY MEAL

The human body needs six kinds of **nutrient** to keep it healthy.
They are:

1 Protein
This helps the body to grow and heals cuts and bruises.

2 Carbohydrate
This gives the body energy for everything it does.

3 Fats
These give energy too. They also keep the body warm.

4 Vitamins
These keep parts of the body working properly.

5 Minerals
These help the body to grow.

6 Fibre
This helps food to be digested.

There isn't one kind of food that has all the nutrients. Most kinds of food have several nutrients. Different foods have to be eaten for the body to get all the nutrients it needs.

The lunchbox meal provided:

	sugar	apple	cheese	bread
Protein			✓	✓
Carbohydrate				✓
Fats	✓		✓	
Vitamins	✓	✓		
Minerals		✓	✓	
Fibre		✓		✓

A meal like the one in this book, which provides all the nutrients the body needs, is a healthy, balanced meal.

Plan some more healthy meals for breakfast, lunch or dinner.

GROUP 1

Eat a small amount

GROUP 2

Eat a medium amount

GROUP 3

Eat a large amount

GLOSSARY

bacteria
microscopic living things which live on other things such as food, and you!

bran
the coat around a wheat germ (see diagram on page 5)

digested
food dissolved in the stomach and intestines of an animal and taken into the blood

dough
a thick mixture of flour, water, yeast and salt

endosperm
the food store in a wheat grain for a new wheat plant to use when it starts to grow (see diagram on page 5)

fungus
a kind of plant which grows on other plants, dead trees and manure

larva
the caterpillar stage in an insect's life

mould
- *a kind of fungus which grows on food and in damp places in the home*

- *a container which is used to shape objects*

nutrient
a substance in food that keeps the body healthy

pesticide
a chemical which kills insects and fungi that harm plants

polythene
a kind of plastic which melts when it gets hot and sets when it cools down

process
the way something is made—it can usually be divided up into stages

rennilase
a chemical which makes milk go lumpy

skimmed milk
milk which has had most of the cream taken out

wheat germ
the new plant in the wheat grain (see diagram on page 5)

yeast
a fungus plant which makes bubbles when it feeds and grows

INDEX